Animal Rights

Barbara James

HODDER
Wayland

an imprint of Hodder Children's Books

Talking Points series
Alcohol
Animal Rights
Charities – Do They Work?
Divorce
Genocide
Homelessness
Mental Illness
Slavery Today

Editor: Jason Hook
Series Editor: Alex Woolf
Designer: Simon Borrough
Consultant: Richard Ryder, Director of Animal
Studies, International Fund for Animal Welfare

First published in Great Britain in 1998
by Wayland Publishers Ltd

This paperback edition published in 2002
by Hodder Wayland, an imprint of Hodder
Children's Books

Hodder Children's Books
A division of Hodder Headline Limited
338 Euston Road, London NW1 3BH

**British Library Cataloguing in
Publication Data**
James, Barbara
    Talking points - animal rights
    1. Animal rights - Juvenile literature
    I. Title
    179.3

ISBN 0 7502 4259 0

Printed and bound in Hong Kong

Acknowledgements
The author would like to thank the following
organizations for their help with this book:
Animals in Medicine Research Information
Centre, Born Free Foundation, Dr Hadwen
Trust for Humane Research (Dr Gill Langley),
Compassion in World Farming, The
Countryside Alliance, International Fund for
Animal Welfare, National Canine Defence
League, People for the Ethical Treatment of
Animals, Royal Society for the Prevention of
Cruelty to Animals, The Vegetarian Society,
World Society for the Protection of Animals.

Picture acknowledgements
Bruce Coleman 6, 52 (Erwin and Peggy
Bauer), 7 (Thomas Buchholz), 10 (Jorg and
Petra Wegner) 22 (Joe Mcdonald), 25 (John
Cancalosi), 54 (Len Rue Jr.); Ecoscene 46
(Robert Baldwin); Getty Images 4 (Art Wolfe),
5 (Kathy Bushue), 11 (Jerry Alexander), 13
(Vito Palmisano), 14 (Mark Joseph), 23
(Michael Rosenfeld), 24 (Martin Rogers), 26
(David Hiser), 27 (Andy Sacks), 31 (G. Robert
Bishop), 38 (Paul Chesley), 40 (Fred
Felleman), 41 (Jan Kopec), 45t (Chip Porter),
45b (Frank Herholot), 48b (Jean-Marc
Truchet), 53 (Renee Lynn), 55t (Frans
Lanting), 59 (John Warden); Impact 15
(Lionel Derimais), 18 (Mark Henley), 32
(David Reed), 35 (Brian Rybolt), 36 (Alain le
Garsmeur), 37 (Roger Scruton), 42 (Mark
Cator), 43 (Otto/Visions), 47b (Colin Jones),
51t (Stewart Weir), 51b (Jonathan Pile); Ole
Steen Hansen 55b; Panos 9 (Sarah Bancroft),
34 (Rhodri Jones), 44 (J.C. Tordai); Polfoto 16
(M. Langkilde); Popperfoto/Reuters 57; Rex
28 (J. Sutton-Hibbert), 56; Robert Harding
47t (Michio Hoshino); RSPCA *cover* (June
Hassall), 8 (Paul Herrmann), 17, 48t (Tim
Sambrook), 19 (John Howard), 21 (Anthony S
Thompson), 49; Sylvia Cordaiy 12 (Jonathan
Smith); Topham 33; Wayland Picture Library
20, 30.

Contents

What are animal rights?

There is a huge variety of life on earth. Nobody knows exactly how many different plants and animals there are, but scientists have estimated that there are between five and thirty million species. Animals come in all shapes and sizes. They live in many varied habitats, from deserts to rainforests. Each unique species is the product of millions of years of evolution. One of these species of animal is *Homo sapiens*, or human beings, and they have had a great effect on the fate of many other species.

How should we treat other animals? Should they be seen as friends, or as products and slaves for our use? Do animals have a right to be treated in a particular way? Do humans have any duty or responsibility to care for them?

What rights does this infant lowland gorilla have? Do humans have a right to kill it for food or display it in a zoo? Should it be allowed to live in its natural habitat?

Many animals behave in similar ways to humans. They care for their young, protecting them from danger and teaching them how to survive in their habitat.

Different beliefs

'Animals, whom we have made our slaves, we do not like to consider our equal.'

Charles Darwin, British naturalist
1809–1882

'The greatness of a nation and its moral progress can be judged by the way its animals are treated.'

Mahatma Gandhi, Indian leader
1869–1948

Rights for animals?

In 1948, the United Nations issued a Universal Declaration of Human Rights. This is a list of basic freedoms and rights that every human being should be free to enjoy. Most countries today try to follow this declaration. Respect for human rights is seen as one of the main features of a civilized society.

Some people feel that animals should have a similar declaration of rights. After all, animals are very similar to humans. They form relationships and care for their young. Animals are intelligent. They feel pain, hunger, fear and pleasure. We believe it is morally wrong to treat other people as slaves or to kill them. Why, then, should we treat animals any differently?

This lioness in Africa has killed an impala to feed her cubs. She must kill other animals to survive. Do you think humans should also kill for food?

Other people argue against animal rights. They believe that humans are more intelligent, and are therefore superior to animals. Other animals kill and cause suffering to obtain food or defend territory. Humans are animals, so why should they act any differently?

Since animals do not seem to understand the concept of rights, why should they be given them? Some people believe that God has given humans the right to use other animals for their own needs.

Human rights and animal rights

The Universal Declaration of Human Rights includes the following articles:
– all human beings are born free and equal in dignity and rights
– everyone has the right to life, liberty and security of person
– no one shall be held in slavery or servitude
– no one shall be subjected to torture or to cruel, inhuman or degrading treatment or punishment.

Animal rights campaigners have written their own declaration of rights for animals:
'We do therefore declare that these animals:
– have the right to live free from human exploitation, whether in the name of science or sport, exhibition or service, food or fashion
– have the right to live in harmony with their nature rather than according to human desires
– have the right to live on a healthy planet.'

Animal Rights Handbook, 1990

Many people now feel that it is wrong to have performing animals in circuses. They say that teaching wild animals to do tricks is degrading.

Animal welfare

It is sometimes claimed that 'animal welfare' has a different meaning to 'animal rights'. Both are concerned with the treatment and suffering of animals, but animal rights movements tend to be more extreme and to question whether benefits to others, however great, can ever justify exploitation.

Animal welfare organizations, such as Britain's Royal Society for the Prevention of Cruelty to Animals (the world's oldest animal welfare group), aim to promote kindness and prevent cruelty to animals. They are involved in reducing the pain and suffering caused to animals in experiments, and in improving conditions for farm, domestic and wild animals.

Animal welfare inspectors investigate complaints about cruelty to animals. They rescue many animals, such as this Moluccan cockatoo.

Animal rights organizations go further in saying it is also morally wrong to use animal products for food or clothing. They oppose the use of animals in experiments and entertainment completely. Organizations such as People for the Ethical Treatment of Animals, in the USA, hope to end the use of animals in these ways. They work towards this by campaigning and protesting, or even by rescuing animals from research laboratories.

Animal rights organizations run campaigns to make their views known to the public and to politicians. These demonstrators are protesting against the use of animals in experiments.

Talking point

'Chimpanzees share more than 98 per cent of our genes, they have complex forms of communication and large stable societies. They use tools, plan for the future and share our emotions.'

The *Independent* Special Report, 28 October 1997.

Do you think it is acceptable for (1) a chimpanzee (2) a human:
– to be operated on as part of a cancer research project?
– to perform in a circus?
– to be hunted for food?

Speciesism

Why is it considered unacceptable to experiment on a human being, but acceptable to do so on a highly intelligent chimpanzee? It is simply because the chimpanzee belongs to a different species of animal.

The philosopher Richard Ryder said: 'To discriminate against beings solely because of their species is a form of prejudice.' This form of discrimination is called 'speciesism'. The term is used to describe the prejudice of humans treating other animals differently from the way they treat other humans. Some people see speciesism as a form of discrimination, just like racism or sexism.

Chimpanzees are very closely related to humans. We consider it wrong to keep humans in a cage. Do you think it is acceptable to cage intelligent wild animals?

Rights for all?

Where do we stop if we do give rights to animals? Do we mean the right to life, or the right not to be caused pain? Do all living creatures have rights? Is it worse to kill a gorilla than a flea? Many questions surrounding animal rights are very difficult to answer. Each person has a different view. Some people will eat fish but not meat. They will kill a wasp but not a bee. How do they decide? It all depends upon what they believe about each animal.

People's beliefs about animal rights come from their family background, education, religion, society and the experiences in their life. Each of us is unique and we have our own unique set of beliefs. Our beliefs form the codes and laws of our society. These in turn affect the way in which the animals in our society are treated.

Different societies have different beliefs. These live ducks are being taken to market in Vietnam. If a farmer did this in your country, would you think it was cruel?

Food and farming

Talking point

'A human has as much right to eat meat as a hawk or a fox does.'

James Cargile,
Ethics and Animals, 1983

'The time will come when men such as I will look upon the murder of animals as they now look upon the murder of men.'

Leonardo da Vinci,
Italian artist and scientist,
1452–1519

Which of these statements do you agree with?

Throughout history and throughout the world, humans have killed animals for their meat. How much meat you eat, and which particular animals you eat, depends very much on where you live in the world. In Western countries, cows, pigs and poultry are usually farmed to provide meat. Other countries have different traditions. In some places, horses, goats and dogs are eaten. In others, wild animals are the only food.

Some people do not eat any meat at all. Many Hindus and Buddhists believe in a code of non-violence, and do not kill any animals for food. A number of people in Western countries are vegetarian because they also feel that it is wrong to kill animals for their meat.

A holy man in India. Many Indian Hindus do not eat meat. They believe it is wrong to kill for food.

Other people have given up meat because they are concerned about the safety of animal products. British beef exports were banned in Europe because of fears that BSE (Bovine Spongiform Encephalopathy) or 'mad cow disease' could be passed on to people. There were a record 100,000 cases of food poisoning in Britain in 1997, causing the British Medical Association to warn that 'all raw meat should be treated as potentially contaminated.'

Many people have become concerned about the safety of meat, especially beef. Inspectors check slaughterhouses and butchers' shops to make sure laws on animal welfare and hygiene are upheld.

A meat diet

In a lifetime, the average person in the USA will eat 23 pigs, 3 lambs, 11 cattle, 45 turkeys and 1,097 chickens.

Should animals be killed for food?

Should we kill animals for their meat? There are a number of arguments to support meat-eaters. Meat provides protein, minerals and vitamins. Humans have eaten meat since prehistoric times, and it seems a natural part of our diet.

Today, most meat comes from farming rather than hunting. Farmers argue that their animals are well cared for. Their needs for food, water, shelter and safety are met while they are alive. If nobody ate meat, what would happen to these animals?

An Irish farmer and his sheep. Sheep need large areas to graze and are not farmed intensively.

Vegetarians argue that a vegetarian diet is healthier. Some also think that it is simply wrong to kill animals for food – humans can eat alternative foods, so they should respect an animal's right to live.

It can also be argued that it is better for the environment to be vegetarian. Livestock farming causes pollution and is not efficient. Ten hectares of land will support 61 people with a diet based on soy beans, 24 with a diet based on wheat but only 2 with a diet based on beef. Fifty times more fossil fuels are needed to produce a meat-centred diet than a vegetarian diet.

Estimated percentage of population who are vegetarian

Country	Vegetarians (% of population)
Estonia	0.20
France	0.85
Germany	4.50
Italy	1.25
Netherlands	4.40
Poland	0.20
Sweden	0.75
UK	5.40
USA	1.00

Intensive farming

Today in Europe, North America and Australia, most animals are reared on large 'intensive' farms. These farms use less land and labour than the more traditional farms. One person can look after 50,000 chickens on an intensive farm. They are very efficient and produce cheap meat, eggs and milk. Intensive farms are often called 'factory farms' because they are designed to mass-produce animals.

Chicks are bred in special units, for their meat and eggs. Since only female chickens lay eggs, millions of male chicks are killed when they are only one day old.

What is it like for the animals?

'Most animals killed for meat spend their brief and miserable lives trapped in hideous, artificial conditions, unable to see daylight or to breathe fresh air.'

The Vegetarian Society, 1994

'We have an outstanding animal welfare record and are very sensitive to consumer perceptions of welfare.'

Meat & Livestock Commission, 1994

Many people, including some farmers, are unhappy about intensive farms. They say that they treat animals as machines, not as living creatures. About 80 per cent of pigs live in concrete stalls. The pigs have no straw bedding and they never see daylight. They cannot move or behave naturally.

These conditions cause sickness. To keep their animals free from disease, farmers often give them drugs and medicines. Some 50 per cent of all antibiotics in the USA are fed to livestock.

The RSPCA believes all consumers have a right to know how animal products are produced. They have introduced welfare standards for animals producing meat, eggs and dairy produce. Where the welfare of animals meets these standards, their products are labelled with the 'Freedom Food' logo. This is the first large-scale welfare labelling scheme in the world.

In 1998, Danish prime minister Poul Nyrup Rasmussen was invited to a pig farm after expressing concern over the welfare of pigs. His criticisms were supported when Danish farmers lost a British order for pork worth millions of pounds because their welfare standards were unacceptable.

Case study

A chick hatches out in an incubator. When she is about eighteen weeks old and ready to lay eggs, she is transferred to the battery unit and put into a cage with a floor space measuring 51 cm x 46 cm.

In this tiny, metal cage, which she shares with up to four other birds, the hen does not have enough space even to spread her wings. In the battery shed, the cages are stacked in rows up to six layers high. There are no windows in the shed. Food and water are piped into troughs in front of the cage.

The hen lays about 300 eggs in a year. These roll on to a conveyor belt, which carries them away. A second conveyor belt takes away the hen's droppings. She has no earth to scratch in, no dust to bathe in, and no place to perch, walk or nest.

Her shed contains about 100,000 other hens. Because she cannot move about or scratch and peck the ground, she pecks at the hens packed in beside her. This leaves them featherless. To stop this, the farmer cuts off part of her beak.

The battery hen lives in such appalling conditions that her claws and feet become damaged, and her bones grow weak and brittle from lack of exercise. A chicken can live for up to ten years. But after only two years, the battery hen is too worn out to lay any more eggs and is killed. Her body is turned into products such as chicken pies, pet food, baby food, soup and stock cubes.

Overcrowding in battery units can cause stress to chickens. They often react aggressively and peck each other.

Pigs on the run

'Police were last night stepping up the hunt for two pigs which escaped from an abattoir minutes before they were due to be slaughtered ... The break for freedom began when three five-month-old pigs went to market at Malmesbury, Wiltshire. One met his fate, but the other two wriggled free, leading their captors on a ten-minute chase around the slaughterhouse.

As they headed towards the river, the men from the abattoir smiled grimly, knowing there was no way across the river, but their smiles turned to astonishment as the desperate pigs leapt into the River Avon and struck out for the other side – their snouts sticking defiantly above the water.'

Kate Watson-Smyth, the *Independent*, 14 January 1998

Live pigs in China are transported to market in home-made baskets. In Western countries they are loaded on to a lorry.

Transportation and slaughter

Before animals end up as packets of meat on supermarket shelves, they have to be slaughtered. Before they are slaughtered, they undertake their final journey. Methods of transportation and slaughter both raise important talking points.

Many farm animals are transported to a livestock market, where they are sold on to a butcher, a meat wholesaler or another farm. Animal welfare groups have criticized many of these markets for treating animals with cruelty and neglect. Animals in some markets are kept in overcrowded pens, injured by sticks or boots and rarely given water.

The transportation of live animals to and from markets and slaughterhouses has led to long-running protests by animal welfare campaigners. Some animals, exported from one country to another for slaughter, face a journey of over 1,600 kilometres. They sometimes have to endure a sea crossing in an overcrowded lorry, without water or food.

Veal crates are banned in Britain because of the cruelty they cause. However, calves are often transported live to other European countries where crates are not banned.

There are laws governing maximum journey and rest times, and the feeding and watering of animals in transit. But not all countries have implemented them. Undercover animal welfare inspectors have gathered evidence which shows that many transporters break these laws. Animal welfare groups argue that long-distance transportation is not necessary, and call for all food animals to be slaughtered as near as possible to their original farm.

Slaughterhouse operations are highly mechanized. Cows are stunned with a fired bolt or electrical stunner before their throats are cut. They are hung up and butchered.

Many animals arrive at the abattoir in a state of fear and distress. Inside the slaughterhouse, undercover inspectors have again found evidence of cruelty and mistreatment – despite regulations concerning animal welfare. According to these regulations, animals must be stunned before their throats are

After butchering, these pig carcasses are kept in cold storage before being taken to shops and supermarkets.

cut. Occasionally, the stunning is not carried out properly and animals regain consciousness before they die.

Like factory farming, the abattoir procedure is highly mechanized, with living animals going in one end and cuts of meat coming out of the other.

The whole process of producing cheap meat or eggs for consumers raises many questions. Do animals, as living beings, have a right to be treated with respect and to die with dignity? The choices are ours. Are you happy to eat cheap meat or eggs produced by intensive farms? Would you be prepared to pay a higher price for animals to have a better life?

Glass walls

'If slaughterhouses had glass walls, everyone would be vegetarian. We feel better about ourselves and better about the animals, knowing we're not contributing to their pain.'

Paul and Linda McCartney

Animal experiments

Worldwide, over 200 million living animals a year are used for research in scientific experiments.

Research goes on in universities, medical schools, commercial laboratories and military or defence establishments. Animal experiments are used to develop new medical techniques. Food additives, cosmetics and household chemicals are tested on animals. Animals are also used in psychological tests, weapons research and space experiments. This research is known as vivisection, which means the painful experimentation with, or dissection of, living animals.

The most commonly used research animals are rats and mice. Scientists also use rabbits, cats, non-human primates (such as baboons and chimpanzees), birds and fish. Most are bred by commercial companies especially for the research laboratory market, although a few are caught in the wild.

Laboratory animals

In the USA, it is estimated that between 17 and 70 million animals are used each year in experiments.

Experiments recorded in the UK in 1996 involved these numbers:

mice and rats	2,190,801
fish	135,165
guinea pigs	103,725
rabbits	53,631
sheep	34,336
hamsters	10,745
horses and donkeys	9,033
pigs	7,389
primates	4,374
cats	1,740

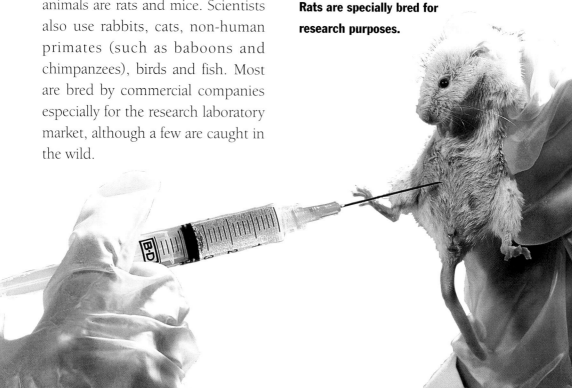

Rats are specially bred for research purposes.

The scientists' argument

Scientists give a number of reasons why living animals are used in experiments. The knowledge of how bodies work is vital to doctors. Experiments on living animals may increase their understanding of disease in humans and other animals. The testing of drugs and other products requires a living body to discover any chemical side-effects.

It is morally unacceptable to experiment on humans. Other animals have a similar biology to us, and they are considered less important and less intelligent than humans. Therefore we use them for experiments. This shows that scientists, and the society which allows these experiments, give humans priority over animals. The benefits to humans are believed to outweigh the suffering caused to animals. Do you agree with this?

This rabbit is being used in medical research. Most laboratory animals are killed and dissected so that scientists can study changes to their body.

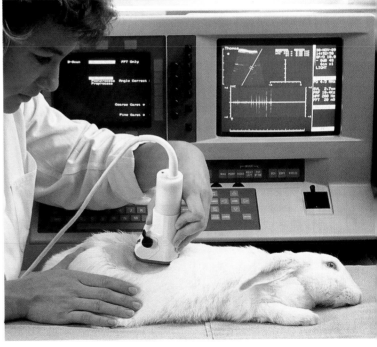

Scientists maintain that experiments are carefully controlled by law, so that animals are well cared for and their pain and distress kept to a minimum. Most countries have laws to control research on animals such as the Animals (Scientific Procedures) Act 1986 in Britain and the Animal Welfare Act in the USA. These laws regulate the handling and treatment of animals in the laboratory, acceptable levels of pain and distress, and standards of housing and maintenance.

23

Acceptable pain?

Many people argue that experiments cause unacceptable pain and suffering to animals. They believe that it is morally wrong to abuse, misuse and kill animals for our own knowledge.

There is evidence that many experiments are unjustified on scientific grounds. Results are often misleading, because animals react to certain drugs and chemicals in a different way to humans. Many experiments test different versions of the same drug. This suggests that far more animals are being made to suffer than is necessary.

This rhesus monkey was used in a famous experiment to see how animals behave if their mother is taken away. It is clinging to a substitute mother for comfort. Do you think this experiment is morally acceptable?

The Bion Project

Monkeys, dogs and rats have all been blasted into orbit, in the cause of the space race. If they do not die in space, most are killed and dissected on their return to earth.

NASA has been particularly criticized for its Bion Project. This was a joint US, French and Russian experiment. Rhesus monkeys were wired up by inserting electrodes into their arm and leg muscles, abdomens and holes drilled into their skulls. After this painful operation, the monkeys were launched into space for fourteen days, restrained so that they could not move. They were part of an experiment to study the effects of weightlessness, yet NASA already had data on human beings who had spent hundreds of days in space.

The project was criticized for its 'lack of scientific leadership and its failure to consider less cruel methods of obtaining data'. After a huge campaign by animal activists, NASA announced the end of its involvement in this project in April 1997.

Medical experiments

We all want to be healthy, and if we are ill we call on doctors to help us recover. Western treatments rely on drugs and surgery. But these are not used on humans until they have been thoroughly tested.

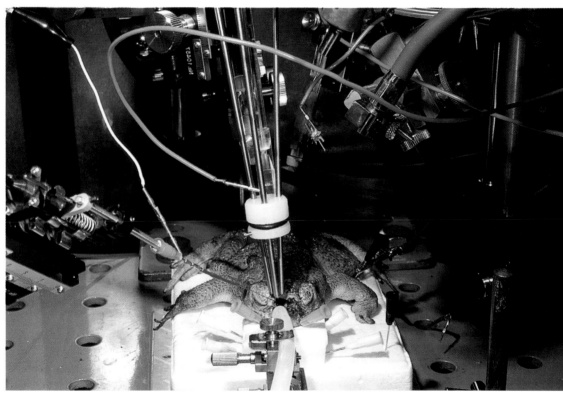

This toad is being used for research into the nervous system. Is it better to use 'lower' animals such as amphibians for research rather than 'higher' mammals such as monkeys?

Because animals do not suffer human diseases, scientists create the effects of disease artificially. To research rheumatism, they use chemicals to inflame the joints of rabbits. To study Parkinson's disease, they deliberately inflict brain damage on monkeys. Thousands of cats and dogs are poisoned with toxins to study lethal viruses and diseases.

Many medical advances, such as organ transplants, antibiotics and vaccines have relied on vivisection. Researchers say that thousands of human lives have been saved by experimenting on animals.

This monkey is forced to smoke before it is given water. People know the links between smoking and cancer, but still smoke. Can scientists justify this animal's suffering by calling it a cancer experiment?

Opinions differ on how much animal experiments have contributed to human health. Some people maintain that improved housing, sanitation and diet have had more effect on human health than medicines. They also point out that testing does not guarantee that a drug is safe. One example is the case of thalidomide, where deformed babies were born to mothers who had taken the thalidomide drug to prevent sickness during pregnancy.

Medical experiments on living animals present some of the most difficult arguments in the animal rights issue. When the health of a person is at stake, it becomes more difficult to say that an animal has equal rights to life.

Are humans more important than animals? Does the human benefit of each experiment outweigh the cost in animal suffering? Is it worth killing hundreds of mice if one human life is saved? Are you more comfortable thinking about experiments with mice than those with monkeys?

Genetic engineering
Genes are found in every cell in the body. They contain the chemical messages, known as DNA, which determine particular characteristics such as the colour of your eyes and the shape of your face.

Genes are passed down through generations, and they are the reason why you can see family likenesses.

Genetic engineering is a technique in which scientists take genes from one living thing, or 'organism', and insert them in another. This alters the genetic structure or 'code' of the second organism, so producing an animal or plant that is potentially more useful to humans.

Scientists have used genetic engineering with pigs to make them grow faster and produce leaner meat. In one controversial case, genetic scientists engineered mice so that they were guaranteed to develop cancer for use in medical research. Genetically engineered animals are known as 'transgenic animals'.

Talking point

'There would not be a single person alive today as a result of an organ transplant or a bone marrow transplant without animal experimentation. All of the work that we did depended on the use of living animals.'

Dr Joseph Murray, 1990 Nobel prize winner for work on transplant surgery.

Would you be willing to undergo an operation if it had not been tested on animals first?

Every animal contains DNA, a substance which carries the animal's genetic information. This mouse sits on a computer printout of its own DNA code. Genetic engineering involves manipulating this code.

Animals by design

Examples of transgenic animals include a 'geep' – half-sheep, half-goat – and a 'cama'. The cama is a cross between a camel and a llama, which was produced in Dubai in January, 1998.

Genetic ethics

'Do we reduce all life to technology? Do we genetically engineer all farm animals? Do we turn them into chemical factories for the production of pharmaceuticals? Or, do we restore our proper relationships and recentralize our values with other creatures?'

Dr Jeremy Rifkin, *Animal Genetic Engineering*, 1995

The number of animals used in genetic experiments is increasing, and genetic engineering is a major international industry. It could lead to a process known as 'pharming', where herds of animals are cloned to mass-produce useful drugs in their milk. A sheep has been genetically engineered in this way so that her milk contains human blood-clotting factor.

Many people feel that it is morally wrong to alter the genetic code of animals. They believe it interferes with the very basics of life and that humans are disturbing the balance of nature. People say that it debases living animals to 'design' them as living factories for human use. There are also concerns that genetic engineering could be dangerous. New species of animal could be engineered which are unpredictable and uncontrollable. Fundamentally, there is concern that genetic engineering causes terrible suffering to the animals involved.

Dolly the sheep, the world's first cloned mammal, meets the press. The news of this scientific breakthrough made headlines around the world, but many people have questioned the wisdom of such experiments.

Case study

Cloning is the technique of producing genetically identical animals. In 1997, scientists at the Roslin Institute in Edinburgh, Scotland, 'cloned' a sheep. To create their clone, the scientists removed the genes of a 'foster' sheep from her egg. To this egg, they then added the genes of an adult 'donor' sheep. This meant that when a lamb was born, she would be genetically identical to this donor sheep. She would be a clone.

Nearly 300 attempts at cloning a sheep failed. According to animal welfare campaigners, many of the cloned lambs that failed to survive also appeared abnormal. Finally, a cloned lamb was born, and given the name of Dolly. She was the world's first mammal cloned from an adult cell. Dolly instantly became an international celebrity. Scientists claimed that Dolly was a breakthrough in genetic engineering. They said that her creation could lead to many benefits for humans, such as the treatment of infertility and inherited diseases.

Dolly's foster sheep was killed six days after her body had been used to produce the lamb. Animal welfare campaigners criticized the cruelty of the

cloning procedure. They also raised another argument against cloning. If a herd of genetically identical animals contracted a disease, they would all react identically. The disease could then wipe out the whole herd.

In January 1998, nineteen European countries signed the first binding international ban on human cloning. The cloning of Dolly had focused opinion against the idea that one day human clones might be created.

Testing cosmetics and household products

Think how many chemicals and toiletries you use at home – shampoo, toothpaste, deodorant, make-up, hairspray and many more. Manufacturers of cosmetics and household products test many of them on animals, to screen the products for possible harmful effects on humans.

There are three main tests. The first is the LD50 (Lethal Dose 50 per cent Test), in which animals are force-fed a product until 50 per cent of them die. The time taken for death to occur shows how poisonous the product is. This test is usually carried out on rats and mice.

The second experiment is the Draize Eye Test. Cosmetics such as shampoo or washing-up liquid are dripped into the eye of an animal for up to seven days. The degree of redness, swelling, ulceration and discharge on the eye is measured. This test is usually carried out on rabbits, because they do not produce the tears which would wash the substance away.

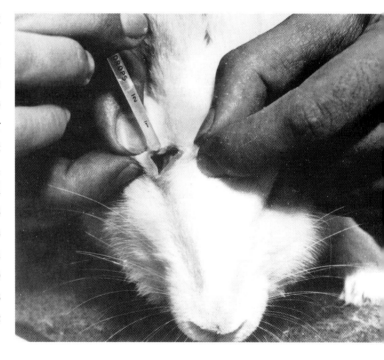

The third test is the Skin Irritancy Test. The skin of an animal is shaved and the product is applied. The skin reaction can then be observed. This test is usually carried out on guinea pigs and rabbits.

Chemicals are dripped into the eye of a rabbit to test for harmful effects which could endanger human health.

Pain for profit

Many famous brands of perfume and cosmetics are tested on animals. A number of supermarket chains and other manufacturers now label products which have not been tested in this way. There are many cruelty-free alternatives on sale from outlets such as The Body Shop.

Manufacturers say that there would be no new products coming on the market without animal testing. Animal welfare campaigners argue that thousands of chemicals and products have already been tested and do not need to be tested again.

While many people do not like medical testing, they can understand the benefits for human health. They can see no possible benefit, however, in causing animals to suffer for beauty products. This type of testing is often referred to as 'pain for profit'. Do we share the manufacturers' responsibility because of the products we choose to buy?

Toiletries such as toothpaste and household chemicals have a more practical benefit than lipsticks and perfumes. Does this make it more acceptable to test them on animals? Would it be immoral *not* to perform these experiments, if the outcome will benefit humans?

This hairless rat looks like something from a horror film. It is actually a real, living creature, bred by scientists for experimentation in their laboratories.

Alternative techniques

There are now many alternatives to animal experiments.
– computers can predict with 80 per cent accuracy whether a chemical will cause cancer
– human cells and tissues grown in the laboratory can be used to research Parkinson's disease and multiple sclerosis
– powerful scanners can research brain disorders, cancer, heart disease and arthritis on human volunteers, without the need for operating on monkeys.

Psychological and defence tests

Psychological tests are carried out in university departments and research laboratories to study the behaviour of animals. Scientists hope that this will increase our understanding of human behaviour. Tests have been used to show how animals are affected by stress, aggression, depression, overcrowding and the deprivation of senses such as sight or taste. Animal campaigners have highlighted grotesque and useless experiments such as deliberately inflicting brain damage on monkeys to see how it affected their ability to travel through a maze.

Animals are also used for research into weapons and warfare. They are subjected to the effects of radiation, nerve gas and biological warfare. Monkeys have been shot above the eye to investigate the damage done by high-velocity bullets to the brain. Anaesthetized pigs have been strapped on to trolleys and shot at close range to test body armour.

After the Gulf War in 1991, an increasing number of animal experiments were used to test antidotes to chemical weapons. Animal welfare groups question the value of such tests. The US Defense Department has itself admitted that their animal studies could not explain illnesses suffered by its troops returning from the Gulf War.

A kitten is used in a psychology experiment. Do you think studies on other animals shed light on how humans behave?

The whole catalogue of human use of animals makes difficult reading. How many experiments are really necessary? Are the results of the work always a positive contribution to human knowledge?

Animals in entertainment

From lions fighting gladiators in ancient Rome to whales performing in films such as *Free Willy*, animals have always been used by humans for their amusement. Today's entertainments involving animals include bullfights, rodeos, horse racing, zoos, aquariums, circuses, films and television programmes. In some entertainments, the animals are highly trained athletes. In others, they are killed, hurt, held captive away from their natural environment or trained to perform degrading tricks.

Do humans have a right to use animals in this way so that we can laugh at them, bet on them, look at them or take pleasure in their suffering? Should we treat animals with more dignity?

A dancing bear entertains a crowd in Pakistan. Animal welfare organizations say teaching animals to perform tricks almost always involves cruelty, fear and punishment. Yet, tourists often encourage such acts.

Bullfighting – art, tradition or torture?

Bullfighting is big business, attracting large crowds and commercial sponsorship. This fight is taking place in Ecuador, South America.

About 35,000 bulls are killed in bullfights in Spain each year. Bullfighting also takes place in France, Portugal and South America. Promoters describe bullfighting as a cultural tradition which combines artistry, skill and courage.

Animal welfare groups argue that the fights are heavily fixed in favour of the bullfighter. They say that before fights, bulls are cruelly handicapped by beatings, confinement in darkness, having part of their horns sawn off, and having petroleum jelly rubbed into their eyes so that they cannot see well. During the fight, the bull is taunted by the matador and impaled with barbed spikes, to weaken him before the kill. The matador tries to kill with one blow to the heart, but this frequently fails and several thrusts are needed before the bull dies. The bulls are not the only victims in the ring. The horses used by the picadors are frequently gored to death or so badly hurt that they have to be destroyed.

About twenty million people a year watch bullfights in Spain, and many of the people who see a fight are tourists. A survey has shown that more than 50 per cent of Spaniards are opposed to the sport of bullfighting, and it is now banned in some towns.

Rodeos

Rodeos began over one hundred years ago in the United States as a contest of skill between cowboys. Rodeo events include bareback riding of horses and cattle, and the roping and wrestling of steers. Today, rodeos are still promoted as a 'Wild West' contest of human skill and daring versus a wild, untamed animal. Rodeo cowboys and promoters say their animals are treated well and are protected by Rodeo Association rules.

Again, animal welfare groups see rodeos differently. They say that the horses and cattle involved are not naturally aggressive, but are provoked or irritated into appearing 'wild'. Electric prods, sharp sticks and straps pulled tightly around their abdomen are used to cause pain and make them buck. The injuries to animals can be horrific, crippling some so badly that they have to be slaughtered immediately afterwards.

A bucking bronco at a rodeo in California, USA. Animal welfare organizations say that horses and cattle are mistreated, but rodeo promoters disagree. Is entertainment ever worth the mistreatment of animals?

Horse racing

While bullfighting and rodeos display obvious signs of cruelty, horse racing has an altogether different image. Elegant, well-bred horses are trained like athletes, to be in peak condition on the day of a race. The partnership between jockey and horse and the intense competition combine to provide a thrilling spectacle.

35

Horse racing is popular with all sections of society, from royalty to the 'man in the street'. Races attract heavy betting and many, such as the Kentucky Derby, are international sporting occasions. Horse racing is controlled by national bodies such as the Jockey Club in Britain and the USA.

However, there have been allegations of over-training, resulting in the early death of young horses. People also claim that the use of drugs to control injuries leads to horses racing when they are not fit. This can cause them to be fatally injured in races. The use of the whip has also been criticized as cruel and unnecessary. The English Grand National has attracted many protests, because its high fences often result in the death of a number of horses.

Horse racing has been called the sport of kings. Many horses are kept in the very best conditions, but there have been allegations of doping and of 'overtraining' of young horses.

Some horses become famous, leading high-profile lives and enjoying happy retirements, but what happens to the horses that don't win? When they do not perform well enough, most are slaughtered for pet food. Horse racing undoubtedly gives a lot of people excitement and enjoyment, but does the sport exploit horses?

Zoos

Most people have visited a safari park or zoo. They are a popular entertainment, especially for children. But zoos also mean captivity for wild animals and because of this anti-zoo campaigners point out their similarity to prisons.

Are zoos educational?

'It is the sadness of zoos which haunts me. The purposeless existence of the animals. For the four hours we spend in a zoo, the animals spend four years, or fourteen, perhaps even longer ... This is not conservation and surely it is not education.'

Virginia McKenna, *Beyond the Bars*

'If zoos are eventually banned it will be a tragedy, because they have so much to teach us, not only as visitors but also as professional students of wildlife. In an ideal world, every child should have the opportunity to visit wild places and see wild animals in their natural habitat. This is clearly not possible.'

Desmond Morris, *The Animal Contract*

It is easy to see the misery of animals kept in poor conditions. Today, more responsible zoos keep primates in spacious enclosures rather than cages.

Zoos are criticized because they keep animals in captivity away from their natural habitat. The animals frequently have too little space or privacy, an unsuitable diet or climate, and no company or family groups. Caged animals become bored. The conditions they live in produce abnormal behaviour, sometimes called zoochosis. This includes swaying, pacing, head-bobbing and biting the cage bars or themselves.

Benefits of zoos

It would be wrong to criticize all zoos and wildlife parks in the same way. Some zoos, particularly in poorer countries, do confine wild animals in tiny cages and terrible conditions purely for profit. Others, however, have breeding programmes for endangered species and keep their animals in large enclosures similar to their natural habitat.

Zoos can educate people about wildlife and conservation, and have an important role in researching animals' behaviour and biology. They conserve species which are under threat of extinction. A large number of zoo animals today are bred in captivity rather than taken from the wild. With many people living in cities, zoos provide a rare contact between people and wildlife. Perhaps this helps to remind people how important it is to safeguard the welfare of our fellow animals.

Is it acceptable to keep small animals such as meerkats in zoos, but not large ones such as polar bears? Is it right to keep wild animals in captivity at all? Do you think that the arguments for conservation and education outweigh those against captivity? How can we make sure that all zoos keep their animals in decent conditions?

Tigers inspect the visitors at a safari park in Seoul, South Korea. There is a growing trend for zoos to keep animals in social groups rather than as single animals in cages.

Zoo statistics

– There are approximately 10,000 zoos worldwide.

– About 1 million animals are held in the world's 1,200 largest zoos. 619 million people visit these zoos each year. 3,000 different species are kept in them.

– 2 per cent of endangered species are registered in breeding programmes. There have been 16 successful programmes to reintroduce animals to the wild.

Orcas are the largest animals held in captivity. In the wild, they live in family groups or 'pods' which communicate in their own language.

Case study

In 1976, a female 'orca', or killer whale, was captured in seas off Iceland. In the wild, she had been living in a family group and swimming up to 160 kilometres a day. Sometimes, the whales had flung their massive bodies up out of the water, as if jumping for joy.

After her capture, the orca was transported to an aquarium in Holland. She was given a name, Gudrun, but now had no family group. She was trained to perform tricks to amuse the public. After eleven years, Gudrun was moved to an aquarium in Florida, USA. Here, she had two calves, Taima in 1989 and Nyar who was born handicapped in 1993.

Gudrun became pregnant again, but after fourteen months of the usual seventeen-month pregnancy she went into labour. The calf was born dead. Gudrun became ill, refusing all food and human attention. She died four days after the birth, after twenty years in captivity. She was the twenty-third orca caught in the wild to have died in this aquarium.

Aquariums are promoted as major tourist attractions. Many people find it more acceptable to keep marine animals captive than land-based animals, but marine mammals such as whales and dolphins are among the largest of all animals kept in captivity.

An orca performing at an American aquarium. In the wild, orcas can stay under water for thirty minutes. Captured orcas are confined to shallow tanks where their natural behaviour is curbed.

There is a growing campaign to ban the use of sea mammals in marine parks and aquariums. Canada, Britain, Israel, Brazil and some states in the USA have all taken measures to prohibit the capture and display of whales and dolphins. Do other sea creatures such as fish, crabs and octopus deserve the same protection?

Hunting

In most countries in the world, people hunt in one form or another. Sometimes, animals are hunted because they are seen as a danger to humans or to domesticated animals and crops. But many animals are hunted simply for pleasure, in what are called blood sports.

Hunters claim that humans have as much right to kill as any other animal. Anti-hunt campaigners argue that hunting is cruel, causing animals great suffering and a violent death. In most societies today, it is unnecessary to hunt for food. Hunting has become a sport rather than a necessity.

Talking point

'Your life may be of no consequence to anyone else but it is invaluable to you because it's the only one you've got. Exactly the same is true of each individual deer, hare, rabbit, fox, fish, pheasant and butterfly. Humans should enjoy their own lives, not taking others.'

Brigid Brophy, author

Is it acceptable to kill an animal:
a) for sport?
b) for food?
c) because it damages property?
d) to make a leather coat?

In Scotland, deer numbers are controlled by 'stalking'. Stalkers pick out an animal from a herd and shoot it with a high velocity rifle. This country sport contributes to the local economy in the Highlands.

A pack of hounds in France prepares for a stag-hunt. Supporters of stag-hunting say it is necessary to cull the deer to protect the environment. Opponents say it is cruel and barbaric.

Hunters say that hunting is necessary to manage wildlife populations, to reduce the damage wild animals do to crops or forest plantations and to stop them preying on farm animals. Anti-hunt campaigners argue that hunting does not control pests. Instead, it alters the natural balance of predator and prey. This allows hunters to justify killing both the predatory animal and its prey. For example, if foxes are hunted, they eat fewer rabbits. The rabbit population then increases and needs to be culled.

Hunters say that hunting helps to conserve the countryside, as wild areas are set aside for animals. Campaigners dispute this. They argue that hunters upset the natural ecological balance by breeding and releasing game animals. To keep these animals safe for the hunt, gamekeepers kill natural predators such as foxes or birds of prey.

Fox-hunting

– In Britain, attempts to introduce legislation banning fox-hunting have prompted mass demonstrations in support of the hunt. Demonstrators insist that in a free society, people should be free to practise a traditional country activity.

– 84 per cent of people in towns and 77 per cent of people in the countryside in Britain disapprove of hunting with dogs.

Gallup, August 1997

Shooting

Shooting is one of the most popular forms of hunting. Many wild species are shot, as well as specially bred game birds such as pheasant and grouse. Shooting is often used to cull wild populations so they cannot cause ecological damage by overgrazing.

In Australia, the shooting of kangaroos for their meat has become an industry. Hunters claim that kangaroos are a pest and cause the land to be overgrazed. Australian animal welfare campaigners argue that kangaroos are not expertly culled, but are shot by amateurs who do not kill them cleanly.

In southern Europe, the mass shooting of birds is a highly controversial issue. Huge flocks of birds fly between Africa and northern Europe on their migration routes. Each year, millions of them are shot or trapped by hunters in France, Spain, Italy, Malta, Greece and Cyprus. There are European Union directives to regulate the numbers of birds killed, but hunting laws are difficult to enforce.

Shooting for fun

'When I was 12, I went hunting with my father and we shot a bird. He was laying there and something struck me. Why do we call this fun to kill this creature [which] was as happy as I was when I woke up this morning?'

Marv Levy,
American football coach

Hunters prepare for a grouse shoot. Hunters say Britain's moorlands would disappear without grouse shooting, as many moors are managed to encourage grouse populations.

Angling

Angling is one of the most popular sports, enjoyed by millions of people. Fish do not express pain like land animals, so for many humans it is difficult to understand that they might be suffering. Animal rights campaigners say that fish suffer physical pain similar to other animals, as well as fear and distress. They believe that even those fish that are caught and released are traumatized and injured.

Anglers argue that fish are either returned unharmed to the water, or are swiftly killed for eating. They also point out the role the fishing community plays in conserving lakes and rivers, and working to reduce water pollution.

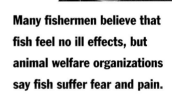

Many fishermen believe that fish feel no ill effects, but animal welfare organizations say fish suffer fear and pain.

Big-game tourism

For the past 200 years, big-game hunters have slaughtered thousands of wild animals in Africa, India and the USA. Hunts were organized to kill elephants, zebras, tigers, lions and buffalo, with the hunters taking home skins, horns and tusks as trophies. This form of hunting has declined, but big game remains an important part of the African tourist industry. Many tourists now hunt only with their cameras, but there are still safaris where tourists pay to shoot wild animals in organized culls. These are often promoted by governments as part of their wildlife management programmes.

'Canned hunting' is another form of big-game hunting in the USA, Canada and African countries. Big game animals are released into a pen where they are shot. The 'hunters' have little hunting to do, and usually shoot the animals from an open vehicle.

A safari in South Africa, where tourists shoot nothing but pictures.

45

Trapping

In commercial hunting, the desire for profit tends to outweigh interest in animal rights. There is a real danger that commercial hunting will result in the extinction of certain species.

Pest control

In the USA, the government offers bounties for the pelts of wild animals to safeguard land for farmers. Wolves, once found in 48 states, are now virtually extinct. The mountain lion has disappeared from the eastern states. In 1991, the Animal Damage Control agency (ADC) killed 1.5 million blackbirds, 96,000 coyotes, 9,000 skunks and over 200 black bears.

Approximately forty million animals each year are trapped in the wild. Many different methods of trapping are used. One particularly brutal device is the leghold trap, which catches an animal's leg in a steel jaw. The trapped animal is left to suffer extreme pain until the hunter returns to kill it perhaps days later.

The leghold trap has been banned in over sixty countries. It is still legal in the USA and Canada, but some states have banned its use. The European Union has passed a directive banning the leghold trap and halting the importation of furs from countries where animals are caught with it. However, fear of a trade war with Canada, the USA and Russia has prevented the European Union ban from being implemented.

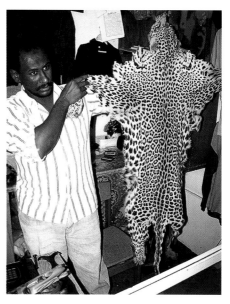

A trader in the Middle East sells a leopard skin. There is a black-market trade in protected species.

Each year in Canada, thousands of baby harp seals are culled. The seals are blamed for depleting fish stocks. In 1996, the Canadian government increased subsidies for the cull. Animal welfare organizations say hunters use illegal methods such as clubbing and skinning alive. There is evidence that the seals are killed for a black-market trade in their furs.

A survey showed that over 70 per cent of Canadians oppose the killing of baby seals.

Case study

Whales have been hunted by humans for centuries. In the late 1800s, the hunt became highly mechanized, using explosive harpoons and fast ships. Commercial whaling took many species to the brink of extinction. Scientists have estimated that the population of humpback whales fell from 115,000 to 10,000 and blue whales from 228,000 to 14,000.

Today, whaling is managed by the International Whaling Commission (IWC). There is a temporary ban on commercial whaling, but countries such as Japan and Norway are pressing to resume large-scale whaling.

Whales are highly intelligent and social animals with their own language. They have been living on the Earth longer than humans. Whales may take twenty minutes to die after being harpooned.

Traditional whaling is not included in the world ban. In Alaska, Inuit people catch whales as they have always done.

Pets

For many of us, our first contact with another animal is with a pet. Animals were domesticated by humans thousands of years ago and the partnership between pets and people has benefits for both. People with pets are loved, entertained and sometimes protected by them. Research has shown that pet owners are less stressed and live longer than people without them. The pets benefit by having food, comfort and safety provided.

Although many of us love our pets dearly, there are question marks over how happy some pets really are. Many animals are kept in an environment which is clearly unsuitable to their nature. For example, wild rabbits and birds are highly sociable creatures. Yet, as pets they are often kept alone in cages. In the wild, fish might swim for many kilometres in a day. But they are often kept in tiny tanks.

The most unpleasant aspect of the relationship between people and pets is the abuse some animals receive at the hands of humans. Animal welfare charities regularly deal with horrific cases of animals neglected or physically abused by people.

The novelist George Eliot once said: 'Animals are such agreeable friends – they ask no questions, they pass no criticisms.'

Birds are popular pets in China. In the wild, they can fly free. Do you think it is right to lock them up in a cage?

Case study

In 1997, an RSPCA inspector visited a woman's caravan. He found her standing in 50 cm of excrement. There were two birds in the caravan and fifteen dogs. A further three dogs were kept in a nearby shed. These dogs had no water and their food bowl was filled with excrement. The floor of the shed was covered with 60 cm of dried faeces.

The animals were removed and taken to a vet. They were found to be underweight and suffering from a number of diseases. One had a tooth growing through its upper lip. Another was suffering from a fractured jaw. Two of the dogs had to be humanely destroyed. The rest of the animals were rehoused by the RSPCA.

The woman was banned from keeping animals for ten years.

A mistreated collie.

Abandonment

Although many people are attracted by cuddly baby animals, they do not always find them so attractive when they grow bigger. Some pets are abandoned because they bark too much or become too boisterous or expensive. Sometimes the owners simply move house or go on holiday, and decide that the pet is inconvenient.

In recent years there has been a boom in the sale of exotic pets. These include snakes, iguanas, scorpions and tarantulas. People often buy them without understanding the animal's needs.

UK pet statistics
– there are 6.9 million dogs and 7.7 million cats in the UK
– in 1996, about 106,000 abandoned dogs were handled by local authorities
– in 1996, 17,000 dogs had to be destroyed

49

Talking point

'Domesticated animals ... can no longer survive on their own, yet they retain many of their basic instincts ... Their bodies and souls yearn to roam but, for safety's sake, they are confined to a house or yard, always dependent on their guardians, even for a drink of water, food to eat, or social contact.'

People for the Ethical Treatment of Animals, *Companion Animals: Pets or Prisoners?* 1997

Are pets willing companions and friends or are they, as some animal campaigners say, slaves for our use and enjoyment?

Exotic pets are not easy or cheap to look after. Many need to be kept at a certain temperature and fed a special diet. They can also grow very big. A rock python, for example, can grow up to five metres long. A large number of exotic pets escape or are abandoned. Many bite or carry disease. Police and animal welfare officers have been called in to recapture Californian King snakes and poisonous scorpions on the loose in city houses.

Many abandoned animals are left to stray, and die through starvation, cold, illness or road accidents. Others are taken to pet shelters where the lucky ones are adopted by new owners. Those that are not chosen quickly enough are destroyed. In the USA, it is estimated that 70 per cent of people who acquire animals end up giving them away, either by taking them to rescue homes or simply abandoning them to fend for themselves.

Pet shops and puppy mills

Despite the large numbers of strays in need of homes, many people buy dogs which have been bred in puppy farms or puppy mills. These are nothing more than factories breeding thousands of dogs for the pet industry. They are bred for quantity not quality.

In the worst cases, puppies are reared in overcrowded and dirty cages. Breeding bitches are continuously producing puppies and are worn out by the age of six or seven. When they are no longer useful, they are destroyed. Puppies are taken from their mothers early, at about four to six weeks of age, and are crated and transported to pet shops.

The popularity of the film *101 Dalmatians* saw an increase in sales of dalmatian puppies. It resulted later in an increase in abandoned strays.

Is there any way of stopping puppies being bred in these conditions? Puppies may be more expensive from reputable dealers, but the buyers can see the condition of the mother and puppies. Alternatively, some people visit pet rescue centres so that they can offer an abandoned dog a good home.

Neutering

Less than 20 per cent of cats and dogs are neutered. Many people do not have their pets neutered, because they believe it makes animals fat and lazy. Neutering does not rob animals of their personality, but it can help reduce the population of stray and unwanted animals. Pets that are not neutered can have litters of puppies and kittens that have no prospect of a good home. One unneutered cat can lead to fourteen million kittens in nine years.

Raining cats and dogs

In the USA, it is estimated that:
- over 2,000 dogs and cats are born each hour, compared to 415 humans
- there are some 54 million dogs and 56 million cats
- over 15 million dogs and cats will be destroyed each year.

Cats for sale in a Chinese market. Many cats and kittens are abandoned and left to fend for themselves.

Exploitation and extinction

Humans are a very successful animal. Perhaps they have been too successful. They have adapted to living in most parts of the world, and have increased their population to nearly six billion. Humans now dominate many other species on earth. This makes them very powerful, but they are not always very wise. Humans have been responsible for wiping out many other species of animal which are now lost to the world for ever.

The human threat

The extinction of a species can occur naturally if it fails to respond to changes in its environment. The dinosaurs are one famous group of animals that died out long before humans evolved. Today, however, extinction rates are increasing. It is estimated that there are between 500,000 and one million animal and plant species under threat. This includes 11 per cent of all bird species.

Human activities have endangered animal species in many different ways. Natural resources have been over-exploited. Huge areas of the world's forests have been felled for timber. Deforestation continues on a massive scale in many of the world's tropical rainforests, especially in south-east Asia and the Amazon basin. The natural habitat of many animals is being destroyed.

Human madness

'As custodians of this planet it is our responsibility to deal with all species with kindness, love and compassion. That these animals suffer through human cruelty is beyond understanding. Please help to stop this madness.'

Richard Gere, actor

Every year more than 210,000 square kilometres of rainforest are destroyed.

The human hunter

Animals have been hunted to the point of extinction. Creatures like the Tasmanian pouched wolf have been wiped out for ever. Even the tiger, one of the most striking of animals, is endangered. It is estimated that the world tiger population has declined by 95 per cent in the last hundred years, and the tiger could be extinct by 2010.

Humans also threaten the oceans. Huge quantities of sharks, dolphins, turtles and birds are killed by fishermen's nets and lines. It was estimated that 40,000 albatrosses are killed each year by tuna fishermen using lines 120 kilometres long with up to 3,000 hooks.

Marine biologist Sidney Holt, of the Independent World Commission of the Oceans, said: 'For every sentence there may be published about … conservation, there will be a page or more about the building of more, bigger and more powerful boats, the construction of bigger nets … Making profit now or soon is the name of the real game.'

Under threat

The Mediterranean monk seal is under threat from hunting, marine pollution and tourist developments destroying its habitat. Its population numbers fewer than 7,000.

Three of the eight sub-species of tiger which existed at the beginning of the century are now extinct.

Sinking life forms

'Most people's knowledge about endangered species is limited to the few (and invariably charismatic) species that have received special attention from zoos, such as elephants, tigers and gorillas. These glamorous species, however, represent only the glittering tip of a huge mass of life forms sinking into the abyss of extinction.'

David Hancocks, Executive Director, Arizona-Sonara Desert Museum, 1994

Under threat

The white rhino of Africa is hunted for its horn and body parts, despite being a protected species. There are about 4,000 white rhinos left, and they face extinction.

Rhinoceroses have been on the earth for about forty million years. They now face extinction because humans hunt them for their horn.

Trade in species

There is an international trade in wild animal species. Minks and stoats are traded for their furs; parrots and tropical fish to stock pet shops; bears, rhinos and leopards to provide ingredients for oriental medicines; monkeys for research laboratories, and all kinds of animal to supply zoos and aquariums.

Many of these animals are trapped in the wild, and have to endure transportation to their new home. Up to 75 per cent of captured parrots and macaws die during this journey. Those that survive face a life that bears no comparison to their freedom in the wild.

Many countries have laws governing the import and export of wild animals. The Convention on International Trade in Endangered Species of Wild Fauna and Flora (CITES) controls the trade in species. CITES bans all commercial trade in species that are threatened with extinction. The Convention has 135 member countries. It has been described as: 'A mini United Nations dedicated to defending the world's most endangered animals, plants and birds from exploitation and obliteration.'

For every bird reaching a pet shop alive, three more have died during capture and transportation. About thirty species of parrot are threatened by illegal trade.

Under threat

There are fewer than 10,000 sloth bears left in India and Sri Lanka. Their forest habitat is being destroyed by logging.

One way of curbing the trade in species is to reduce demand from consumers for products such as furs, crocodile-skin bags and oriental medicines. Do you think that you have a role to play in refusing to buy such items?

The market for the ingredients of traditional Chinese medicines threatens many species. Some suppliers no longer deal in body parts from endangered species such as the tiger and the rhino.

Case study

In China, Asiatic black bears or 'moon bears' are milked for the bile in their gall bladders. The Chinese trap the bears and keep them in cages on bear farms. The cages can be so small that the bars touch the bears on all sides.

When the bears are milked, they are roped into a corner of the cage to stop them struggling. A metal tap is implanted into their stomach so that they can be milked regularly. This procedure is so painful that the bears cry out when the bile is removed.

About 8,000 bears are thought to be farmed for their bile. It is used in Chinese medicine where it is believed to cure jaundice, high blood pressure

There is an international campaign to reduce the number of bears farmed for their bile.

and infections of the intestine (all conditions which can be treated with other medicines). The bile is very expensive, with a bottle costing up to £1,000. Bear farms also have a sideline in bear paws which are made into a very expensive and exclusive soup costing about £250 a bowl.

In the wild, these bears live in the forests of northern and central China. They are protected by CITES, which China signed in 1981. However, within China the bears are only in the Class II protection category. This means that the bile trade is allowed to continue.

The International Fund for Animal Welfare is campaigning to end this practice, and has reached agreement with the Chinese government and medical profession that no young bears will be tapped for three years. They are also funding research into herbal alternatives to bear bile.

Campaigning for animals

There are many ways in which governments can protect wild animals. They can set up areas such as nature reserves, national parks and wilderness areas, where wild species and their habitats are protected. Environmental and wildlife concerns can be taken into consideration when planning for housing and city developments. Laws can be strengthened regulating the protection of wildlife and curbing the trade in endangered species.

Individuals can also make a difference. Many people help animals in their spare time. There are a large number of organizations people can join.

Rescue workers in Australia try to help a humpback whale calf, which became trapped in shallow water after it had swum into a shark net.

Some organizations deal directly with animals, for example by rescuing injured animals or cleaning oil from sea birds. Others use the media and letter-writing campaigns to try to change laws and improve conditions for laboratory or farm animals.

The list on page 63 of this book gives addresses for some of the major organizations, many of which have special youth groups and can offer information and educational material.

Under threat

The whooping crane is killed by hunters when migrating between Canada and the southern Americas. There are less than 250 surviving.

Conserving wildlife

'Most of us are raised with the belief that man is the most important and most intelligent animal on earth. We believe we are superior to other animals and have a right, even duty, to subdue and use them for our own benefit. As a species we are not accountable to any other on this, 'our' earth. It comes as a surprise and a shock to many of my students when they learn that few animals depend on us, but that we depend on many of them for our continued existence.'

George Small, College of Staten Island, in *Project Interspeak*, 1979

People can also show their concern for animal welfare through what they eat and buy. Some choose to eat less meat. Others buy meat and eggs from free-range or organic farms. Labelling schemes mean it is possible to buy only those cosmetics which have not been tested on animals.

There are many reasons to conserve wildlife. Animals are essential in controlling other animals and maintaining the natural balance between species. Some species are valuable to humans for the products they give us such as medicines, clothing and food.

The world will be a poorer place for us all if we cannot share it with other animals from the smallest ant to the most magnificent gorilla.

Some animals we find beautiful or fascinating. We tend to think of conserving animals because of what they mean to us. Perhaps they should be conserved because they have as much right to exist on the earth as we do?

Glossary

Abattoir A slaughterhouse.

Battery A series of cages for intensive breeding of poultry or cattle.

Bile A fluid which aids digestion, and is secreted by the liver and stored in the gall bladder.

Bounties Rewards paid by the state, for example for the culling of animals.

Clone An animal that is genetically identical to its 'parent'.

Conservation The protection and careful management of natural resources and the environment.

Cull Reduce the numbers of animals in a herd or population.

Directives General instructions issued from a single authority.

Discrimination Unfair treatment of someone or something, based on prejudice.

DNA Deoxyribonucleic acid, which is present in nearly all living organisms, and carries their genetic information or 'genetic fingerprint'.

Doping Giving drugs to race horses to affect their performance.

Electrodes Components which can conduct electricity.

Exploitation Making use of something for one's own needs.

Extinction The complete elimination of a population or species.

Fossil fuels Fuels such as oil, coal and natural gas.

Genes Units containing DNA which define an animal's characteristics and inherited features.

Habitat The natural home of an animal or plant, such as a woodland or a desert.

Intensive farms Farms where animals and animal products are mass-produced.

Livestock Cattle, horses, poultry and other animals which are kept for domestic use but not as pets.

Meerkats Small, burrowing African mongeese, who live in social groups.

Migration The movement of an animal to change its habitat according to the changing seasons.

NASA National Aeronautics and Space Administration, the US space agency.

Neutering Castrating or spaying an animal to prevent it reproducing.

Pharming The use of genetically engineered animals to mass-produce medicines or drugs.

Picadors In bullfighting, people on horseback who torment the bull with lances.

Primate A type of mammal which includes monkeys, apes and humans.

Psychological tests Experiments which investigate behaviour or thought.

Recentralize Restore to a central or balanced position.

Resources Any materials which are useful to humans such as oil, wood, fish and metals.

Species A group of animals or plants that can breed with one another. For example, all domestic dogs can interbreed because they are the same species but they could not breed with a fox which is a different species.

Sponsorship The payment of funds by a person or group to support an activity, for example funding by manufacturers and advertisers to support sporting events.

Steers Castrated bulls.

Thalidomide A drug used as a sedative, but found to cause deformities in the foetus if taken by mothers during early pregnancy.

Ulceration The forming of sores or ulcers.

Veal crates Small wooden cages in which calves are kept before being slaughtered for their young meat.

Vivisection Vivisection originally meant 'to cut up while alive' but it now refers to all experiments on live animals.

Books to read

Animal Rights by Mark Gold
(John Carpenter Publishing, 1995)

Animal Rights: a Question of Conscience
ed. Craig Donnellan (Independence
Educational Publishers, 1997)

*Finding Out About Animals in Medical
Research* (Hobsons, 1995)

The Pocketbook of Animal Facts and Figures
by Barry Kew (Green Print, 1991)

Save the Animals by Ingrid Newkirk
(Angus and Robertson, 1991)

The Teenage Vegetarian Survival Guide
by Annouchka Grose (Red Fox, 1992)

Why Animal Rights? (Animal Aid, 1996)

Why Do People Harm Animals?
by Miles Barton (Franklin Watts, 1995)

*The Young Person's Action Guide to Animal
Rights* by Barbara James (Virago, 1992)

Publications of the RSPCA Education
Department, RSPCA, Horsham,
West Sussex

Sources

Beyond the Bars ed. Virginia McKenna,
Will Travers & Jonathan Wray
(Thorsons, 1987)

Ethics and Animals by James Cargile, ed.
Miller & Williams (Humana Press, 1983)

The Animal Contract by Desmond Morris
(Virgin Books, 1990)

The Animal Rights Handbook
(Living Planet Press, 1990)

Animal Genetic Engineering
by Dr Jeremy Rifkin (Pluto Press, 1995)

Animal Life (RSPCA, Autumn 1997)

Companion Animals: Pets or Prisoners?
(PETA, 1997)

*Cruelty or Culture? A special report with the
World Society for the Protection of Animals*
(The *Independent*, 28 October 1997)

Life on Earth by David Attenborough
(Collins, 1979)

Useful addresses

Animal Aid
The Old Chapel, Bradford Street,
Tonbridge, Kent TN9 1AW
Internet: http://www.envirolink.org/arrs/

Animals in Medicines Research
Information Centre (AMRIC)
12 Whitehall, London SW1A 2DY

Born Free Foundation,
Cherry Tree Cottage, Coldharbour,
Dorking, Surrey RH5 6HA
Internet:
http://web.ukonline.co.uk/bornfree

British Union for the Abolition of
Vivisection (BUAV)
16A Crane Grove, London N7 8LB

Compassion in World Farming (CIWF)
Charles House, 5A Charles Street,
Petersfield, Hampshire GU32 3EH
Internet:
http://www.ibmpcug.co.uk/~ciwf

Dr Hadwen Trust, Humanity in Research
22 Bancroft, Hitchin, Hertfordshire,
SG5 1JW

Food and Farming Information Service
The National Agricultural Centre,
Stoneleigh Park, Warwickshire
CV8 2LZ

International Fund for Animal Welfare
(IFAW)
Warren Court, Park Road, Crowborough,
East Sussex TN6 2GA
Internet:
www.easynet.co.uk/ifaw/home.htm

League Against Cruel Sports
Sparling House, 83-87 Union Street,
London SE1 1SG
Internet:
www.lightman.co.uk/lacs

The National Anti-Vivisection Society
261 Goldhawk Road, London W12 9PE
Internet: http://www.cygnet.co.uk/navs

National Canine Defence League (NCDL)
17 Wakley Street, London EC1V 7LT

Royal Society for the Prevention of Cruelty
to Animals (RSPCA)
Causeway, Horsham, West Sussex
RH12 1HG

The Vegetarian Society
Parkdale, Dunham Road, Altrincham,
Cheshire WA14 4QG
Internet: http://www.vegsoc.org/

World Society for the Protection of
Animals (WSPA)
2 Langley Lane, London SW8 1TJ

Index

HAVERING COLLEGE OF F & H E

128416